The Genius of

Albert Einstein

An Albert Einstein biography

Michael Woodford

Introduction

Albert Einstein is the most recognizable face of science.

The man who created the theory of relativity, alongside so many other breakthroughs in the world of physics, though, was so much more than just a scientist.

A philosopher, musician, humanitarian. A pacifist.

Einstein was never a man to back down in a fight, and never one to accept the words of authority if they were unjustified, or harmful to others.

The kindly, white haired old man, was a flawed genius. A man who possessed excellence in science, a deep love for humanity, struggled in his personal life.

This is the story of Albert Einstein, the greatest intellect of the twentieth century, perhaps of all time.

An Independent Spirit – the Early Years

March 1879 will not go down as a particularly notable month. On the 29th, British troops defeated 20,000 Zulu warriors in the Battle of Kambula.

A couple of moderately known sportsmen were born – George Wilkinson, an English water polo player, and Waldemar Tietgens, a German rower.

But neither are even close to being household names.

Yet it was a good month for scientists. In a twelve-day period between the eighth and twentieth, no less than three intellectuals to be were born. People who would bring about significant change to the way we view the world.

Otto Hahn would win the Nobel Prize for his work in discovering nuclear fission. Maud Menten would become a significant player in the discovery of an immunization against scarlet fever.

But neither of these, great scientists though they would become, could imagine the successes the middle of the three future scientists delivered that month would achieve.

Because on March 14th, 1879, Albert Einstein was born.

The world into which the genius emerged was that of a new country. Germany had only been in existence for eight years.

Ulm, in the south west of the newly named country, with its splendid cathedral and broad sweep of the River Danube would be home for just six weeks of the baby's life, before the family moved to the much larger city of Munich.

The country had formed only in 1871, when the Prussian aristocrat and German Chancellor Otto von Bismarck took power.

Although a democracy (men had the vote) most power lay with Bismarck, and he set about forming alliances with previous empire leaders to retain his authority.

This was a period of huge growth. The new state was established and within nineteen years, Germany was arguably the strongest country on mainland Europe.

Albert's parents were Jewish, but not especially religious. In fact, his father described the religion as akin to ancient fairy tales.

Hermann Einstein was an engineer and a salesman. In Munich, he founded a company with his brother which made electrical equipment.

Perhaps it was Hermann's genes and interests that sparked the young Albert's fascination for discovery.

Hermann was interested in maths and sciences at school, and was good at them, but his family were not wealthy. Rather than study on past his schooling, he left to begin work as a merchant.

Indeed, his early career saw him gain expertise in this field, and he became a partner in his cousin's business in Ulm.

There, he was in charge of selling bed feathers.

The company in Munich saw him as the salesperson, whilst his brother, Jakob, looked after the technical side of the business.

They moved it to Italy in 1894, but the business struggled and closed, costing the family their livelihood.

Without his brother this time, Hermann moved the family once more to set up a new venture in Milan.

This fared better, but Hermann found the strain of running the business considerable, and in 1902, at the age of just 55, he suffered heart failure and died.

Just prior to working in the bed feather business, his fancy had been tickled by a young lady called Pauline Koch.

She was just 18 when the two married, and three years later Albert was born.

Pauline had been a daughter to poor parents who made good. Her father would later become 'Royal Wuerttemberg Purveyor to the Court', which meant that he provided goods to German royalty.

As a consequence of her parents' new-found position, Pauline received a good education, and was keen on the arts.

She was a talented musician, expert in the piano. She encouraged young Albert to take up the violin at the age of just five.

When the family moved to Pavia in Italy, she would be separated from Albert as he continued his education in Munich.

The separation was hard for her – Albert was just fifteen at the time.

After her husband's death, Pauline moved in with her sister and her family, travelling with them as they moved around Germany.

She fell ill with cancer during World War One, and as her life faded, Albert (by then married) took her from the sanatorium to spend her last few months with him.

But these events are long in the future. Young Albert has just been born – Germany is undergoing exciting, but uncertain, times and he has moved to Munich were his father and brother have set up their new electrical business.

When Albert is just two years old, a new addition joins the family.

Maria, Maja as everybody calls her, will become his closest childhood friend.

She would go on to write a biography of her brother in 1924, revealing secrets of their formative years.

Included amongst these were his early encounters with the piano, inspired and driven by his mother's musicianship, the fact that his grandmother thought him too fat.

And his mother's view that his head was too large – she may not have realized at that point that it contained a somewhat larger than normal brain.

Albert had his first identifiable brush with science when he was around the age of four.

When his father showed him a compass, the youngster was not especially taken with its shiny frame, or mysterious markings.

It was the fact that wherever he stood it always pointed north that fascinated him.

Albert started school at the age of six. Although he and his family were Jewish, that they were not practicing meant that they were able to enroll him in a well-regarded Catholic school in Munich.

Petersschule had an excellent reputation for academic standards, against which Albert flourished.

However, as is the case with many of the brightest children, he found discipline hard to accept.

At the time, military activities featured highly in German schools, even ones for children as young as Albert.

He could not come to terms to being instructed, however, and would wander off to play his own games, and construct models from card.

When he was ten, Albert moved to the Luitpold Gymnasium in the city.

This was a highly academic school, and was difficult to get into. However, its curriculum was centred on classical learning, such as in Greek and Latin.

Maths and sciences, the fields that most fascinated young Albert, were considered less important.

Albert, though, was resourceful, and developed his interest in learning outside of the school environment.

His uncle Jakob was, of course, an engineer, and would set him mathematical problems and, for a treat, algebra.

A young doctor friend of the family lent him books on philosophy and modern science.

As he started to close in on his teens, Albert became almost obsessed with his religion.

Off his own back – his parents remained distinctly uninterested in the subject – he learned and observed kosher eating habits.

He read the Torah extensively and created his own hymns to God.

He took up preparation for his Bar Mitzvah but, half way through his studies, he suddenly lost his certainty in religious belief.

Perhaps as a result of his growing understanding of scientific matters, perhaps because of the influence of his parents, he abandoned religion.

In fact, like many zealous converts who become disillusioned, rather than adopting simple disinterest, he developed a strong resentment towards all forms of organized religion.

Like a more advanced response to his younger self's feeling towards military instruction, he fostered a vehement opposition to the kind of dogma with which religion is often associated.

When the family moved to Italy to further their business ventures, Albert joined a boarding house to continue his studies at the Gymnasium.

However, rather like his mother, the separation caused him unhappiness. He persuaded a doctor to write him a note diagnosing 'neurasthenic exhaustion'.

This gave him the excuse he needed to rejoin the family. It also meant that he would escape military service.

On arriving in Italy, he declared to his rather surprised parents that he was going to renounce his Jewish faith.

They were even more shocked when he announced that he would do the same for his German citizenship.

The teenaged Albert Einstein was certainly a young man who knew his mind.

He also knew that he would study to gain a place at a highly academic technical institute, the Federal Swiss Polytechnic in Zurich, where he would specialize in physics.

The future Nobel prize winner and probably greatest mind of the 20th century took the exams.

And failed.

Learning Difficulties and Academic Successes

Enter many schools and before long you will come across a particular department.

This section of the school will often be brightly decorated – the sort of place a young person will find interesting and stimulating to visit.

And frequently, these places will display photographs of Albert Einstein and other well known, but disparate, people.

You will have entered the learning support department of the school. These sections have been called many things over the years – special needs departments, further learning centres, the tutorial section and so forth.

But they each exist to support students who suffer from one of a number of barriers to learning.

The most common of these is dyslexia.

This condition makes reading and writing more than doubly difficult. Sufferers find it very difficult to visualize words in their mind and on the page.

As a result, spelling becomes a real problem – in serious cases writing becomes effectively illiterate.

Reading is also problematic. One of the effects of the condition is a kind of bouncing effect on words. They move around on the page in the eyes of the dyslexic.

The condition is incredibly common, around one in eight boys and one in twelve girls experience suffer from dyslexia.

Usually this is in a mild form, but it can be devastating educationally. Even today, we are still learning about the condition.

It appears to be hereditary, passing especially down the male line, and sometimes skipping a generation or two.

For many years, dyslexia sufferers were considered backwards in their learning. For considerably more, their condition was completely unknown.

Albert Einstein suffered from dyslexia, although, during his time, he would not have known this.

He is in good company. To return to the learning support department of our school, alongside Einstein's picture, several others will be posted.

Pablo Picasso is likely to be there. The business billionaire Richard Branson is another well-known and extremely successful dyslexic.

Film director Steven Spielberg, Mohammed Ali and actor Tom Cruise are others in this category.

We now know that sufferers from dyslexia often, but not always, develop interests in visual and practical subjects.

In fact, those that require the least writing. When putting pen to paper is a considerable chore, it makes sense to be more interested in areas of school that minimize the need to do this.

However, back in the late 1800s, the idenitification of dyslexia was a long way off.

Clearly, the Polytechnic recognized something within Albert that identified his potential, if not his academic performance as measured in tests.

The Principal suggested that Albert should not give up, but rather spend a year in a Swiss school preparing to retake the exam.

Albert chose to do so, and spent the year lodging with one of the teachers, Jost Winteler, and his large family.

Apparently, he got on well with his hosts, especially the seven children, and had a great year.

Having always been a little aloof, quiet - although with his stubborn streak, he seemed to change over the course of that year, turning into a confident, chatty young man.

Re-taking the exam, he passed with ease into the Zurich Polytechnic and embarked on a four-year teacher training programme.

At the end of this, he would be qualified to teach physics and maths at a high school.

His four years, though, were spent on the bread-line.

He lived in student digs, albeit in one of the city's more middle-class areas, and survived on a monthly income of 100 Swiss francs, which was provided, mainly, but his mother's parents.

It seems as though his decision to follow a teacher training degree might have been driven by his family's financial position at the time.

His father's and uncle's business was struggling, and money was extremely tight. Albert would have felt it important to follow studies that led to a career, so that he could earn and add to the family coffers.

However, his first love was physics, and he continued to study extensively at the Polytechnic.

He spent time with the lead physics' professor, Heinrich Weber. The two would work in the professor's lab, where electrical engineering was the teacher's main area of expertise.

For Albert, however, the learning quickly became frustrating. He found that Weber, as a scientist, was old-fashioned, and disregarded most modern study of the time. In fact, he began to fall from favour with his lecturer.

As a result, he went back to what he knew best, and supplemented his studies by learning independently out of the curriculum time offered by the Polytechnic.

He also worked with Hermann Minkowski, his maths lecturer – the teacher would later play an important role in Einstein's theory of relativity.

But in his independent studies, Albert read widely – consuming both established works and new theories in physics.

He established a close and long-lasting circle of friends whilst at the Polytechnic.

Amongst these were Michele Angelo Besso, whom he met through their shared love of music.

Besso was interested in philosophy, and was especially influenced by the works of the Austrian philosopher Ernst Mach.

Mach's beliefs were grounded in fact, rather than spiritual speculation, and Albert became himself under their spell. Later, the beliefs of Mach would play a role in Einstein's theory of special relativity.

Another close friend was Mileva Maric. Mileva was a Hungarian student, and three years above Albert in their studies.

She was not especially brilliant, but was a hard-working student, and the two began to develop a close bond.

Although Albert was popular with the ladies, this relationship took on a greater intensity, and shortly after graduation, she told Albert that he had made her pregnant.

Albert wanted to marry her immediately, but this caused problems with his family, who felt that Mileva was below their own social standing.

Although the Maric family eventually approved of the proposed union, it did not happen before the child was born.

Little Lieserl was taken in by Mileva's parents, and put up for adoption. Sadly, little more is known about the girl.

The only other evidence, which is little more than a theory, came to light in Michele

Zacheim's enlightening but controversial book, 'Einstein's Daughter.'

The author conducts a painstaking search for any evidence of the young girl in what is now Serbia, where Mileva's parents lived.

She concludes that the girl may not have been adopted. No evidence for such an occurrence can be found, although Zackheim admits that the war-torn region is not an easy place to trace official records, especially those dating back over a century.

However, she concludes that a more likely outcome for Lieserl Maric Einstein is even more tragic than abandonment by her family.

The young girl may have contracted scarlet fever in her infancy, and died before she was two years old.

She may also have been mentally disabled possibly, Zackheim claims, because her mother was infected by Einstein with syphilis, which affected the girl's development in the womb.

She is unable, though, to offer much evidence for this claim.

Albert and Mileva would eventually marry, but more of this later.

To return to Einstein's friends from his polytechnic days, a third is also of significant note.

Marvel Grossman was a native Swiss, the son of a successful Zurich factory owner, mathematics student and confirmed liberal.

Albert and Marcel were close, with the scientist relying on his friends notes for exams – Marcel was a year older.

The friendship would prove long lasting. Marcel helped Albert to secure a job after Polytechnic, and also contributed his mathematical expertise during Einstein's work on the general theory of relativity.

Albert graduated in August 1900. Two of the four who graduated in his discipline at this time immediately gained work teaching at the Polytechnic.

Albert was not so lucky. Professor Weber was German, and did not approve of the student who had given up his citizenship, and who regarded the professor's own work as old fashioned.

So rather than being in a position to immediately contribute to the family funds, Albert found himself living back with his family.

He decided to continue his studies, working on his doctorate which focused on the kinetic theory of gases. He funded this work through taking part time teaching jobs.

His reputation began to become known during this period, when three of his papers were published in the well-regarded publication 'Annalen der Physik'.

In the papers, Einstein espouses the current thinking dominating Physics. This was called the mechanical worldview, and was based of the works of Newton.

In brief, the theory was that all matter was made up of particles (later named atoms) which existed within Newton's three laws of motion – action and reaction, force and acceleration and finally inertia.

Albert found these theories limiting, and unable to explain some the of the phenomena he was finding out about.

Never being one to shy away from an opinion, particularly when it challenged established thinking, he was happy to express his views, and the created considerable interest amongst the scientific, academic community.

These early papers, although later discoveries demonstrate that they held flaws, tackled and established a general molecular theory of heat.

That heat flow, or thermodynamics, could be understood in terms of Newton's theory of movement.

The papers also gave an indication of the philosophy underlying much of Einstein's later works – that there was unity between different aspects of physics.

Rather than being a disparate collection of theories, physics could be seen as an inter-linked whole.

Having attempted, and failed, to find work as an assistant to an established scientist, he worked for a short time as a teacher in a nearby town,

Albert tried to fund himself working as a tutor to an English boy in Schaffhausen, a town close to Zurich.

But these temporary jobs lacked security, and could not fund the work that Albert increasingly wanted to explore.

With the help of Marcel Grossman, his college friend, he moved to Bern to begin work in a patent office.

The office was run by a colleague of Marcel's father.

His job, which carried the princely salary of 3500 Swiss Francs, was to assess the legitimacy and practicality of various inventions which passed through the patent office.

He was good at this, which meant that he not only secured a rapid raise in his salary, but he also had enough time to carry out his own scientific studies.

He established a close circle of friends, including some from the Polytechnic. These young people shared a fascination for philosophy and physics, met regularly and called themselves the Olympia Academy.

But a personal event was to change the direction of Albert's life.

Towards the end of 1902, Hermann Einstein suffered his heart attack. Albert rushed to Milan to see his dying father.

Close to the end, Herman finally agreed to the marriage of Albert and Maliva.

Marriages

With his family's blessing now in place, Albert set about marrying his college sweetheart.

On January 6th 1903 they were wed in a civil ceremony in Bern.

Life was good. Albert was earning a comfortable salary and soon another child was on the way – this time a boy.

Hans Albert Einstein was born, and Albert initially paid lots of attention to looking after his son, and helping Mileva.

Unfortunately, the support was short-lived. It was the turn of the 20th century, and it was the woman's job to look after the children.

But Albert did more than just work at his day job. His scientific studies were taking up more and more of his life.

In 1905, when young Hans was still a toddler, Albert had his 'miracle year'. A burst of activity in his love for science meant even more time away from Mileva and Hans.

Mileva struggled to cope, and suffered from post-natal depression. The house became dirty and messy, and although Albert tried to help, his commitment was to his other love – science.

He would carry out his research, scribbling equations on a pad, as he held the baby.

He was also a terrible flirt – always popular with the women, Albert seemed unable to keep his eyes away from other ladies.

However, Mileva battled on, and in 2010 their second son was born. Eduard's birth signaled an improvement in their relationship for a while, but it did not last.

Mileva once more became depressed, and Albert once more became obsessed by his work.

Then, in 2011, things became even worse when Albert accepted an offer from the University in Prague.

Mileva, depressed, concerned about her husband's flirting, with a new baby – they called him 'Tete' - and a young child, disliked the city intensely.

It did not work out, and perhaps that was why after just a year, Albert accepted an offer from the Zurich Polytechnic where he had studied as a student.

Mileva was delighted to be returning to a city with which she was familiar, and where she at least had friends and acquaintances.

But Albert was not one for settling. His parents had moved about a lot when he was a child, and he was taking this to further extremes.

With a reluctant family in tow, the University of Berlin called, and he was off. It was now 1914, War was in the air and Berlin was not the friendliest of places.

Mileva's Hungarian background made her a target for abuse from the German people in Berlin.

Tensions were everywhere. But there was also another issue that was causing her alarm.

Albert's cousin Elsa lived in Berlin. And Mileva had suspicions that their relationship could be more than just a family one.

Her fears were founded, and Albert started to see his cousin more and more regularly. It signaled the end of his first marriage, because he and Mileva argued incessantly.

Finally, he moved out of the family home, and she took the boys back to Zurich. Albert drafted a contract stating the support he would offer and then, in 1916 when he was visiting the boys, he asked her for a divorce.

The always fragile Mileva descended into complete depression, made worse by her trying to cope with Eduard, who was proving exceptionally bright, but incredibly difficult to manage.

Although he read Goethe and Schiller when still very young, had a photographic memory and learned with astonishing speed, emotionally he was a troubled boy.

The divorce hit him badly, but the support of Mileva and his love of music helped him to a successful educational career, and a chance to study his chosen field of psychiatry.

But, by the age of 20 emotional troubles had transformed into full scale mental illness. Eduard suffered from schizophrenia.

Mileva tried to care for her beloved son, but his condition deteriorated and he had to be entered in a psychiatric sanatorium in Zurich.

He was in and out of the 'Burgholzli' for the remainder of his life.

When Maliva died, exhausted in 1948, Eduard spent some time with foster families, but in 1957 he entered the sanatorium for another temporary stay.

However, this time her remained there until his early death in 1965.

Hans, Eduard's elder brother, also took the divorce of his parents badly. Mileva took on a lot of his education, and he successfully entered a career as an engineer.

He married Frieda Knecht in 1927, and that marked an upturn in his relations with his father, which had become strained after the divorce.

They had four children, but tragedy struck when their second son, Klaus Martin, died from diphtheria when just six.

More horrors hit the family when, in 1939, another son – David – was born. He died aged just one month.

With just their first child – Bernhard – still alive, the couple adopted a daughter, Evelyn.

Frieda died suddenly in 1958, and Hans remarried. His new wife was a doctor – Elizabeth Roboz. They had no children.

In 1937 Hans followed his father to the US. He left his family behind, but returned to Zurich at the beginning of 1938, before the entire family emigrated to the US later that year.

After the war, Hans settled down to a job as professor for hydraulics at the University of California.

He remained there until retirement in 1971, and died two years later, from heart failure, on July 26th, 1973.

As for Mileva, following her divorce from Albert, her life became devoted to her Tete. She died in Zurich in 1948.

Albert's relationship to Elsa had started in childhood. As his mother's niece, Elsa and Albert grew up together – Albert even living for a time in their house – but had lost contact in adulthood.

The relationship was reborn in Berlin, and quickly developed.

Elsa was a fine cook, and had also looked after Albert when he had been seriously ill with stomach problems in 1917.

But the extent of the love between them is open to question. Although they married just three months after his divorce to Mileva was finalized, it seemed to many to be a marriage of convenience rather than romance.

At the same time, they had shared romantic letters when he lived in Zurich.

Else was 43 at the time of their union, and Albert three years younger.

She had been married before, to Max Lowenthal, and they had three children, although her one son had died in infancy.

Albert became, though, a father figure to her daughters, Lise and Margot, Lise working as his secretary for a spell. However, more on this relationship shortly.

To some of Einstein's colleagues, it appeared that Elsa was seeking some kind of reflected glory in her husband and cousin's fame.

But whilst Mileva had actively helped her husband with his research, Elsa provided a role as a good housewife.

If the relationship was purely platonic, as seems to be the case, then her cooking and housework created an environment in which her husband could work easily and successfully.

By the 1920s, Albert had established himself as a world-famous figure. His wild hair and 'mad professor' demeanor becoming as popular as his science.

This made him even more attractive to certain women, and his eye for the lady had not deserted him as he grew older.

Even though there may not have been a sexual element in his marriage to his cousin, nevertheless, his antics caused unpleasant gossip. Elsa was not pleased.

She wrote the following to a friend about her husband's wanderings: '…such a genius should be irreproachable in every respect. But nature does not behave this way, where she gives extravagantly, she takes away extravagantly.'

However, whether familial or otherwise, Albert seemed to hold Elsa very dear to his heart.

In 1935, they emigrated to the United State, and she quickly developed heart and kidney problems.

Albert devoted himself to her during this period, and was devastated by her death on December 20th, 1936.

He said afterwards that 'I have got used extremely well to life here. I live like a bear in my den. This bearishness has been further enhanced by the death of my woman comrade, who was better with other people than I am.'

A series of letters discovered by his granddaughter throws light onto Albert's own feelings around his love life.

It is ironic that a man who devoted his career to simplifying the study of physics should live in such emotional turmoil.

Even early love letters to Mileva have elements of the bizarre. They would share loving thoughts and comments interspersed with analysis of complex mathematical formula.

His cold side also came through in some of these letters. During his dissolving marriage to Mileva he wrote – not discussed or argued but wrote:

'You will make sure that my clothes and laundry are kept in good order; that I will receive my three meals regularly in my room; that my bedroom and study are kept near, and especially that my desk is left for my use only.'

It should be remembered that Mileva too was an academic – not as earth-shatteringly able as her husband admittedly – who had supported and helped him in his work towards his greatest discoveries.

He further wrote that she should end any personal relations with him (he is still her husband at this point), stop talking if he requests and should not expect any intimacy.

Other letters reveal a disturbing thought process in Albert's mind. It appears as though he was uncertain whether to marry Elsa, because he also proposed to her daughter, who was also his secretary, Lise.

It seems as though Albert had many affairs, but whilst seeking the relationships he appeared annoyed by them at the same time.

In another of his letters to Elsa he writes that they 'shower him with unwanted affection.'

Evidence of either startling honesty or that their marriage was completely platonic is found in other letters.

He happily reports of relationships with women called Estella, Toni and Ethel. Others he refers to just by their initials, such as M and L.

He even talks about his 'Russian spy lover' who is called Margarita.

The mysterious M is thought to be a Berlin socialite, Ethel Michanowski, with whom he was involved in the late 1920s and early 1930s.

She was around fifteen years younger than Albert, and friends with his stepdaughters.

Whether good news of bad, he states in another 'Out of all the dames, I am in fact attached only to Mrs L, who is absolutely harmless and decent.'

That letter must have made Elsa feel much better!

He even involves his step-daughters in his affairs, on one occasion asking Margot to forward 'a little letter for Margarita, to avoid providing curious eyes with tidbits.'

Letters also challenge some of the views that he was cold towards his sons and first wife Mileva. Perhaps he, as he admitted after

Elsa's death, just found communicating his feelings through the spoken word difficult.

After all, this was a characteristic of the young Albert.

His affection for Elsa is also revealed in the letters, which are held by the Hebrew University, in Israel, an institution Einstein helped to found.

The letters showed that, although he was frequently away from home lecturing and touring around Europe, he wrote nearly every day.

Another letter, not from the collection held by the Hebrew University, offers deeper insight into Albert's view of relationships.

The letter was sent to a friend in 1953. She had discovered that her husband had been having an affair.

In it, he described monogamy as a bitter fruit, and one that 'most men (as well as quite a number of women) are not… endowed by nature.'

He argues that when conventions – we assume he means marriage – put restraints on natural human impulses, those impulses (i.e., to have affairs) become even more powerful.

Although this letter was written when he was in his seventies, it is possible to see traces of the teenager who renounced his Judaism and the small boy who fought against military drills in school.

He had not changed a lot.

Indeed, it seems as though he had developed his own moral code when it came to man/woman relationships.

Some evidence exists that his marriage to Elsa was prompted by concerns from her parents. They felt that conclusions may be drawn from Albert's attentions which could harm her daughters.

Albert, on the other hand, prescribed to a view that, if it was enjoyable and caused no harm, then anything was acceptable.

This moral code, which he developed, was quite self-serving, and allowed himself to be seen as the victim.

He said that affairs usually led to the man being caught between two women, and those two women would grow to hate each other.

That was, he argued, tough for the man to take!

Another example of his desire to put his own interpretation on his extra marital activities can be found in another of his, remarkably indiscreet, letters.

He writes of his relationship with Mrs L (Austrian Margarete Lebach): 'She didn't tell you a word. Isn't that irreproachable?'

He also felt that women should accept adultery, as long as the man continued to care for his wife.

'You should be able to respond to his sins with a smile, and not make a case of war out of it,' he wrote.

But, whilst he could deal with complex scientific problems, the world of relationships seemed beyond him.

He saw things in simple terms – man was by nature polygamous, and conventions made polygamous activities harmful to others.

He saw no satisfactory conclusion to the problem.

But perhaps this attitude towards relationships covered his own inability to be honest with his own feelings.

He made a significant and revealing comment when hearing of the death of his life-long friend, Michele Besso.

Speaking to Besso's son, he said:

'What I admire in your father is that, for his whole life, he stayed with only one woman.

That is a project in which I grossly failed. Twice.'

Annus Mirabilis and the Nobel Prize

If Albert Einstein thought he was a failure when it came to marriage, then the same cannot in any way be said when it came to physics.

In 1921, at the age of 42, he was awarded the highest honour possible for a man in his field – the Nobel Prize for Physics.

The specific citation stated that the award was: '…for his services to Theoretical Physics, and especially for his discovery of the law of the photoelectric effect.'

He received the prize in 1922. This was as a result of a strange quirk in the legacy left by Alfred Nobel.

He laid down certain criteria for the award of his prize, and the awarding committee did not feel that any physicist met these standards in 1921.

However, Einstein's work was by now world famous, and the conditions laid down by Nobel allowed an award to be presented the following year where none was awarded in the previous one.

In that situation, Nobel's criteria changed slightly, and Einstein's work was able to meet these.

He was, of course, prolific in his studies, producing numerous theories. Here we will look at some of them.

And, as we shall see, four of the most famous of these were discovered in a very short period of time.

Photo Electric Effect

In this, Einstein identified that light does not always travel in waves, as was the established belief.

Instead, he identified that sometimes light traveled as individual particles. And, each of these particles carried a 'fixed' amount of energy, called a quantum of energy.

To the everyday person, such a revelation can seem a little under-whelming, but in fact it challenged the entire way in which physics was regarded.

For the first time, it presented a serious alternative to the concept ofNewtonian mechanics – it proved that they were not the whole story.

Theory of Relativity

It is often a surprise to those whose interest in physics is merely peripheral that it was not his theory of relativity for which Albert Einstein won his Nobel Prize.

Whilst working at the patent office in Bern, Albert realized that Newton's law of gravity, whilst usually accurate, did not always apply.

When objects were very large, and very distant, different laws seemed to operate.

Firstly, his theory consisted of two parts, the Theory of Special Relativity and the Theory of General Relativity.

The first of these, in simple terms, determined that all movement is relative to other objects. As an example, somebody in a deep sleep is (mostly) stationary.

However, viewed from distant space, that sleeping person is travelling virtually at the speed of light.

If you are on a moving train, then another train catches you up and moves at an identical speed, it seems as though you are not moving at all.

The Theory of Special Relativity also determines that the speed of light is always constant. Very recently, this theory is coming under challenge, as scientists work on ways to increase the speed of light.

However, that research remains in its early stages.

The Theory of General Relativity redefined the way Mankind considered gravity. It showed that, when objects are immensely distant, it is impossible to tell what causes their change in motion.

Provided the perspective is from a moving object itself, it is impossible to tell whether another, distant, moving object is moving as a result of the gravitational pull of a further object.

Or as a result of inertia.

This theory also determined that large objects cause space to bend, and that the extent of the bend was dependent on the weight of an object.

For example, a child's wooden block on a piece of thin card would cause the card to bend.

However, if the block is replaced with a larger, heavier one, so the card bends further.

The notion that space was an object capable of change, rather than an inanimate entity, was revolutionary in its scope.

Brownian Movement

Albert's development of the theory of Brownian Movement occurred during his 'annus mirabilis' of 1905; the year in which his scientific discoveries took him away from his wife and young son, Hans.

It was also the year in which he discovered his Nobel Prize winning theory of light, and his theories of relativity explained above.

Brownian motion is the name given to a discovery by an early 19th Century biologist, Robert Brown. He observed pollen particles executing apparently random motions when they floated on water.

He observed the same with dust particles, which meant that these movements were not any sign of life, but the result of some force.

Albert Einstein took the theory further, identifying that molecules in fluids moved randomly.

This meant that an individual, minute particle would, in a short period of time, receive random impacts or random strength from random directions.

And it was this that caused the random movements that Brown observed.

E=MC2 The Theory of the Relationship Between Mass and Energy

The final astonishing discovery by Albert during the year of 1905 was perhaps his most famous.

Indeed, the equation that describes his theory of the relationship between mass and energy is frequently identified as the most recognized in the world.

And, it is the theory that forms the basis for nuclear energy.

The theory works means that energy released from an object is equal to the difference in mass of an object, times the speed of light, and squared.

So, for example, when an atom is split into two, the combined weight of the two new pieces is less than that of the original.

And that difference in weight has been released as energy.

Another way of looking at this is to consider that nothing can disappear. However, it can change state from matter to energy.

Matter is energy in an organized form, and energy is matter in its disorganized state.

The application to splitting the atom (which of course post-dated Einstein's theory) is clear.

As the atom splits, energy is released. When that energy is focused, nuclear energy is created. That energy can be channeled for good, as in nuclear power, or for bad, as in nuclear weapons.

Physical Cosmology

Einstein took his General Theory of Relativity further in 1917, applying it to the universe as a whole.

His findings proved unsatisfactory to him, and it was many years of study before, in the 1920s, he founded a theory of the universe that we hold today.

That it is in a constantly changing state, growing and shrinking.

He had observed this back in the early days of this work, but had been initially uncomfortable with such a radical theory.

Not least, because it begs the question of what exists beyond this universe, a philosophical and spiritual question which would have been uncomfortable to set at the time.

He therefore developed a statistical theory, which he called 'static universe' or the 'cosmological constant', however the theory never sat comfortably with him, and he eventually abandoned it in favour of the changing universe we now believe is the case.

Although, in 1931, it seems as though he returned to the theory of the 'cosmological constant' arguing that there is a continuous creation of matter.

Something that would challenge his $E=MC2$ theory.

Albert Einstein is behind far more scientific theory and discovery than just the ideas listed above.

Amongst much else, he created a fridge that does not use greenhouse gases. Scientists are returning to his creation to see whether it is capable of mass production as a way of reducing the greenhouse effect.

He was a major driving force behind the Manhattan Project (to which we will return later). This was the US Military project to create the atom bomb.

Indeed, he was active in the world of theoretical science throughout the overwhelming majority of his life.

To the United States

Anti-Semitism – hatred of the Jewish people – was rife around the time of Albert's birth and childhood.

In the 1890s, a specific movement in Germany tried to popularize anti-Semitism amongst the population as a whole.

But that movement failed, and by the early 1920s Germany was considered one of the best countries in Europe to be Jewish.

By this time, although the Jewish numbers in Germany equaled just one per cent of its population, eighty per cent of those were German citizens.

Many had married Germans, and converted to Christianity; and a large number had fought on the German side during the First World War.

They were prominent and successful in business, the arts and politics, and many were extremely wealthy.

Given the backdrop of the impositions placed on the German population by the Treaty of Versailles, they were an easy target for hatred.

It was during the 1920s that race scientists first began to postulate about the superiority of the Aryan race, which they called 'Herreras'.

They felt that this master race was superior to those they identified as 'Untermenschen', which means sub human.

These groups included black people, and Roma gypsies.

However, the Jews had a class of their own under this racist set of beliefs, they were called 'Gegenrasse'.

Or, not at all human.

As Adolf Hitler's profile in post First World War Germany grew, he targeted the Jews as responsible for many of the country's problems.

He saw them as an ungrateful, money grabbing group who operated outside of the best interests of their home country.

Hitler came to power in 1933, the year Albert Einstein finally emigrated to the United States, along with his wife, Elsa. Even though he had abandoned his religion, nevertheless he was still categorized as a Jew.

He had begun to sense the danger Jews faced in Germany. Although his lectures and publications had made him famous, and wealthy, he had also experienced vitriol and attacks.

He was also aware that restrictions would soon be placed on Jews who were working in Germany, and realized that the most prominent members of the race could well be the first to suffer.

It would become firstly very difficult, and later impossible to continue his research.

Stepping aside from the history for the moment, we of course know with hindsight that his predictions were soon to come true.

It is astonishing, and indicative of how a nation can come under a dictatorial spell, that one of the greatest men in the world would be subject to such ill treatment.

Einstein avoided the worst of the atrocities carried out against the Jews, but only just. He missed the brown shirts 'persuading' Germans to boycott Jewish shops.

He avoided the anti-Semitic posters that began to flourish. He escaped the civil rights denying Nuremberg Laws or 1935, and the restriction from becoming professionals.

And he was in the United States at the time of Kristallnacht – the night of the broken glass – when synagogues, homes and businesses where destroyed, and Jews attacked and put into concentration camps.

But for all this, although comparisons are impossible to draw such was the suffering of Jews, life in the United States was not all plain sailing.

Albert had first visited the country back in the early 1920s. He had embarked on a lecture tour in 1921, landing in New York.

He was greeted by Henry Fine, a senior officer at Princeton University, and gave five lectures there on his theory of relativity, which he had recently returned to and developed.

He also made his first tentative steps towards Zionism whilst in the US, meeting with the Zionist movement in the country.

The movement sought to create a homeland for the Jews, a protected nation in what is now Israel.

From New York, Albert undertook a tour of the Eastern and Mid-West United States which was more like a modern-day series of rock concerts than a scientific expedition of enlightenment.

He was such a figure – perhaps emphasized by his wild hair and 'mad-professor' looks – that crowds greeted him madly, like the genuine superstar he was.

It was not normal for a scientist to be so treated.

His motivation for the tour was initially financial. He thought that he could provide financial security for himself and family, who were living in Zurich at the time, through the tour.

But he set his price to high, and initially the Universities rejected his proposal.

However, he was persuaded to go to the States after Kurt Blumenfeld, the German Zionist leader, visited him in Zurich.

He brought with a telegram from the world leader of the organization, asking that Einstein would accompany him, Chaim Weizmann, on a fund-raising tour of the country.

This would raise funds for a Hebrew University in Jerusalem, and promote the settlement of Palestine.

Initially refusing to be associated, Einstein then decided that, as a Jew, he had a duty to support the movement.

The decision was not universally well received. Despite the fact that Germany was, at that time, safe for Jews, many had long memories.

Several had renounced their heritage and fully assimilated into German life. They, including his friend Fritz Haber, thought that such a well-known name as Einstein becoming associated with the Zionist movement would restart questions about the loyalty of Jews to Germany.

Haber tried to dissuade his friend, but Albert saw the opportunity of re-establishing Germany at the heart of the world's scientific movement, which would come from the attention his tour would create.

This first visit was largely a big success. Twenty thousand fans greeted him in New York, and at every stop on his tour he was overwhelmed by his welcome from the public.

But two signs were forerunners of some of his later experiences on returning to the US more permanently.

He was snubbed by Harvard University, and regarded with extreme caution by many American Jewish leaders.

Back to the 1930s where a concerned Albert Einstein arrives in the United States for the second time, on this occasion he is accompanied by Elsa, his second wife.

It is December 1930, and he has accepted work in California. After the furor of his first trip, nearly ten years earlier, this time he aims for a quieter stay, but this proves fruitless.

Cheering crowds and visits to numerous important events and people mean that his arrival, which was in New York, is as tumultuous as his previous trip.

He travels to California to meet the president of the University in which he is to temporarily teach, but Einstein's pacifism contrasts badly with Robert A Millikan's patriotism and belief in militarism.

His pacifism leads Einstein to meet with many fellow thinkers, including Charlie Chaplin and head of Universal Studios, Carl Laemmie.

Then, in February 1933, he visited the US once again.

As well as his considerable discomfort at the way things were going in his homeland, he had accepted a further, temporary professorship at the California Institute of Technology.

This had meant him leaving his role at the Berlin Academy of Sciences, although he would return after his two months stay in California.

But Hitler came to power at the end of January, 1933, and changes were felt immediately.

Albert and Elsa returned to Europe in March of 1933, landing in Belgium. But they discovered that their home had been raided and their sailboat sold.

The house would eventually be converted into a Hitler Youth Camp.

Einstein formally renounced his German citizenship, handing in his passport, and learned that he had been declared a target for assassination.

The Einsteins stayed in Belgium for a while, before moving to England and then on once more to the US.

In April of that year, he discovered that, almost without any fuss, Jews had been barred from holding any official positions, which included teaching at Universities.

There had been virtually no objection from the lecturers' colleagues.

Then, his works were targeted by the German Student Union, and were burned, whilst the Propaganda minister, Joseph Goebbels stated:

'Jewish intellectualism is dead'.

He was listed in a magazine as an enemy of Germany, under the phrase, 'Not Yet Hanged', and the magazine offered a reward to anybody who would kill him.

He arrived in the US for this, his third visit, on October17th 1933 having secured a position at the Institute for Advanced Study.

This was initially for six months, but unsurprisingly, he had many other offers to consider. These included opportunities to work at Oxford University, in England.

Anti-Semitism at this time was not unknown in the United States. Whilst not of the scale in Europe, it was still present.

In England, the Einsteins had received armed protection against attacks from pro-Nazi anti-Semites, and in the US many universities, including Princeton, had strict quotas.

The result was they contained almost no Jewish lecturers or students.

His known pacifism was also a cause for anger by some officials in the US, something that would escalate later.

But, despite all of this, in 1935 he chose to apply for citizenship to the US, and remain there permanently.

The Manhattan Project and Pacifism

Albert Einstein was an outspoken pacifist and anti-racist.

So much so that he came to the attention of the then Head of the FBI, J Edgar Hoover.

He identified Albert as a possible communist, and certainly 'an extreme radical.' The accusations would not have meant much to Albert, because as we know, he had always regarded authority with skepticism.

Whether as a boy disputing military activities at school, or in the laboratory challenging established viewpoints, like all great thinkers, he felt that those in charge existed, in part, to perpetuate themselves.

'Unthinking respect for authority is the greatest enemy of truth,' he said back in 1901, when just into his twenties.

But the campaign against him by the FBI was a serious one. It continued for over twenty years, even carrying on for a short time after his death.

And ran to over 1800 pages.

Author Fred Jerome's book, 'The Einstein Files', reveals the extent of the attempts, led by Hoover, to see the scientist arrested as a political subversive.

He was even considered a Soviet Spy. It seems as though a clash of personality was behind Hoover's (not untypical) attempt to bad mouth the Nobel Prize winner.

Hoover believed in obedience to instruction, and to maintenance of order. These principles were, as we now know, anathema to Einstein.

The FBI tapped Albert's phone, checked his trash and opened his mail in attempts to discover incriminating evidence.

They knew that he was violently opposed to, and prepared to speak about, injustices and civil rights violations.

As we have seen, it was known by the time that Einstein planned to move to the US in the 1930s that he was a supporter of peace, and was prepared to aid organizations which held similar views.

He was also in sympathy of the Zionist movement (he would later be offered the Premiership of Israel, but declined the offer). He was passionate about politics, and supported military disarmament.

And because of this, the Woman Patriot Corps was the first organization to publicly oppose his entry to the US, arguing that he should be denied this option

The letter from the Corps is the first entry into his FBI file.

Such was the extent of the (failed) attempt to by the FBI to discredit him, that they went as far as to bug the house of his secretary's nephew.

They also compared him to Stalin, stating that even the Soviet Union leader was associated with fewer anarchic and communist groups than the world's leading physicist.

But although Albert was very opposed to war and unthinking obedience to decisions made by those in Authority, he nevertheless contributed much to US society in the 1930s.

One of his most significant actions was his role in the Manhattan Project.

The project began when three chemists discovered a way of splitting the uranium atom in 1938.

As we know from Einstein's earlier works, when an atom is split, energy is released. In the case of the uranium atom, the amount of this energy is phenomenal.

Enough to create an enormous bomb.

But although they knew how to split the atom, the feasibility of creating a controllable and usable bomb from this was hard to estimate.

Einstein discovered that the Germans might discover the answers to this conundrum, he urged the US President, Franklin D Roosevelt, to make the creation of the bomb a key priority.

He did this against his own pacifist leanings.

Astonishingly, in hindsight, the US Army Intelligence office excluded Einstein from working on the project, denying him the necessary security clearance.

They further restricted any access to him from scientists working on the project.

This was because of his left leaning politics – presumably stressed by the FBI.

Certainly, if the US authorities had at that time possessed a nose, they would have cut it off to spite their face.

Roosevelt listened, though, to Albert Einstein's arguments, and did indeed make the Manhattan Project a key wartime priority.

However, when the first atomic bomb was dropped on Hiroshima on August 6th 1945,

Albert was devastated by what he had helped to create.

'Woe is me' he is alleged to have cried.

Although, as he often protested, he had no involvement in the creation of the bomb itself, he recognized that it was his ground-breaking research that led to even the concept of a nuclear weapon to take hold.

And that by arguing to Roosevelt about the urgency of beating the Germans to the creation of this weapon of mass destruction, he had speeded up its invention.

He always protested that, had he known the Germans would not succeed in developing the technology for nuclear weapons during the war, he would not have advocated it to the President.

We can only speculate on how the world would look without the bomb, but we do know that the Nazis were closer to the creation of this devastating than thought at the time.

Germany's own scientists, including Otto Hahn, had made significant steps along the road towards their own bomb, using a variant of uranium.

Fortunately for the Allies, the leadership of the Nazi dictatorship were more interested in diversifying their weapons development.

With the V1 and V2 rockets, plus the utilization of the jet engine, nuclear options were put on the back burner.

Einstein's pressure on Roosevelt was important in winning the race for the first nuclear weapon.

His Later Years

As a physicist, Einstein's greatest years were in his twenties, thirties and forties.

These were the times he produced his finest works.

The later years of his scientific life were spent trying to find one further great achievement, his 'unified field theory'.

Einstein's long held belief was all of physics was interlinked. He went some way towards proving this with his discoveries of 1905, but his attempt was to explain all of the laws through just one mathematical model.

He was unsuccessful in his search, but his theory is still the holy grail for physicists today, as they continue to search for this model.

By the end of the war, the white haired, mad looking scientist we know and love so well had become Albert Einstein.

It enabled his reputation to grow at a speed that continued despite lack of progress in his professional, scientific life.

He was associated with pure genius, added with a touch of eccentricity and a soupcon of everybody's favourite grandparent.

But this persona hid a still active and determined desire to achieve a mark politically.

With his pacifism to the fore, he continued to protest against many sensitive issues. The Cold War was one of these.

He worked happily with scientists from the Eastern Bloc, and was an advocate for both socialism and global unity.

This meant that he held a deep opposition with the West's anti-communism, 'Red Scare' politics.

He defended friends who were communists against the McCarthy witch hunts that began to proliferate.

These were not the moves associated with the kindly old man image that the public wished to, and continued to, hold.

His membership of some radical civil rights groups – defending the views and promoting the rights of a wide range of minorities – caused anxiety amongst political leaders.

His FBI file grew quickly.

Albert's Zionism grew apace with his opposition to right wing politics in the United States. He was a determined and loyal supporter of the new state of Israel.

But in typically contrary fashion, he was also an arch opponent of the Jews' right-wing militia – led by Menachem Begin – that developed through the 1948 Israeli War of Independence.

He wrote to the New York Times, attacking Begin as responsible for the massacre of Palestinian people in the village of Deir Yassin.

He called the leader a 'fascist' and a 'terrorist'. However, he was supportive of the socialist leader David Ben Gurion, who would become Israel's first independently elected Prime Minister.

Indeed, it was Ben Gurion who invited Albert to become the country's President in 1952 – an offer the scientist turned down.

It seems, though, that Ben Gurion had been a little duplicitous in offering the role, which was a mostly honorary one.

He later wrote: 'I had to offer the post to him because it's impossible not to. But if he accepts, we are in for trouble.'

At the time, Albert was considered the greatest living Jew, but the thought of becoming a figure head and a politician in the later years of his life was one with which he simply did not feel comfortable.

He liked his freedom, and enjoyed the opportunity this gave him to be controversial.

'I am deeply moved.' he said of the invitation 'by the offer from our State of Israel and at once saddened and ashamed that I cannot accept it.'

Chaim Weizmann – he who had been behind Einstein's first tour of the United States in 1921 had been the first President.

That the offer should be made so soon after
the Holocaust, and the War of Independence,
to be the figurehead of an emerging and still
unsettled State was a mark of the regard held
for Albert Einstein.

In these, his later years, he was a true icon.
He represented not only huge intelligence
and unparalleled wisdom. But also, deep,
meaningful humanitarianism.

In 1954, as his life began to draw to its close,
Albert reflected on his time. His adopted
country was, to somebody for whom the
rights of humanity were paramount, a mess.

Economically, it was thriving. Its people
were the consumer kings of the world.
Manufacturing was at its peak, expendable
wealth almost unimaginable.

New technologies were making people's
lives easier. A young Elvis Presley was about
to change the face of youth culture.

But not for everybody. If you were black, or gay, or left leaning politically, then you were among that group considered 'un-American.' McCarthy was after you.

At this time Albert wrote a letter published in a magazine in which he considered whether he would wish, if he had his time again, to be a scientist.

He decided that he would not. No doubt with a mixture of typically irony and a deeply felt sense of powerlessness in the face of the prevailing political winds, he declared that he would come back as a plumber.

'I would rather choose to be a plumber of a peddler in the hope to find that modest degree of independence still available under present circumstances.

This triggered some wit from the plumbing community. One worker, a Stanley Murray who was based in New York, wrote to him.

'Since my ambition has always been to be a scholar and yours seems to be a plumber, I suggest that as a team we would be tremendously successful' he penned.

'We can then be possessed by both knowledge and independence. I am ready to change the name of my firm to read: Einstein and Stanley Plumbing Co.'

As amusing as the exchange might be, underpinning Einstein's comments were deep concerns around freedom of speech.

He believed, with justification, that the ability of academics and teachers to work freely and openly had been compromised.

Led by Senator McCarthy, and his lies, many political leaders and much of the media had jumped on the right-wing bandwagon.

Academics and teachers, non-compliant aspects of the press, Government workers, those in the arts – all were at risk of ruin if they spoke out.

To disagree with McCarthy was to be un-American. For somebody so opposed to dictatorial rule as Albert Einstein, such conditions were unbearable.

McCarthy was a charlatan from the outset. In 1950, he claimed to have a list naming 205 State Department workers who were members of the Communist Party.

When pushed, the list seemed to always be somewhere else.

However, a senate committee was created to investigate the claims, and later declared Joseph McCarthy's accusations:

'…perhaps the most nefarious campaign of half-truths and untruth in the history of this republic.'

Despite this, Republicans had not run the White House for sixteen years, since the end of the depression.

They ran with McCarthy's lies, offering him a platform to shout about his perverted view of American society.

They even organized a doctored picture showing the leader of the Senate engaged with the leader of the US Communist party.

But the American public responded well to the accusations, and the Republicans won a great victory in 1952, winning the White House, Senate and House of Representatives.

McCarthy was rewarded with the position of Chair of the Subcommittee on Investigations; his power was now unchecked and his lies given the authority of his position.

As we saw earlier, many groups fell under his attack, but the teaching profession, to which Albert Einstein was committed, was one of his main targets.

It was said at the time, by a former University chief: 'The entire teaching profession in the US is now intimidated.

In 1953, a teacher, William Frauenglass, was called to appear before the Senate subcommittee.

The crime the Brooklyn High School teacher had allegedly committed? Six years' previously he had led a training course for teachers.

Organized by the Board of Education, it had focused on ways in which teachers could work to ease cultural and racial integration, thereby reducing tensions in schools.

In the McCarthy led US, such a course was 'against the interests of the United States.'

Frauenglass needed help, and turned to the 'incorrigible nonconformist' fellow teacher, Albert Einstein, somebody to whom he felt enormous respect.

Still at Professor at Princeton at this time, Albert was now regarded not only as the world's greatest living scientist, and certainly the most famous, but also a committed anti-racist and anti-war activist.

Albert obliged, writing an open letter in which he stated categorically that fear mongering from politicians was suppressing freedom of speech and freedom to teach.

He declared that, unless they would be completely submissive to the will of the Republican politicians, then teachers had no future.

He went on, speaking directly to the victim of the Senate committee's allegations, to say that he felt the Brooklyn teacher should refuse to testify any further.

'This kind of inquisition,' he continued 'violates the spirt of the Constitution.'

Albert declared that he was happy to go to prison for his beliefs, because somebody had to speak out against the outrages taking place in the world's most powerful nation.

Frauenglass followed Einstein's advice, refused to testify, and lost his job.

However, Einstein's views, coming from the mouth of such an eminent man, stung McCarthy.

With the deep disrespect typical of arrogance and narrow mindedness, he said that he did not care whether the speaker's name was 'Einstein or John Jones' but somebody who spoke out as Einstein had was an 'Enemy of America.'

The country's true enemy went on to describe Albert Einstein as 'disloyal' and 'not a good American.'

Yet even in this, his final years, Albert loved a fight. He said that McCarthy led practices had 'become incomprehensible to the rest of civilized mankind and exposed our country to ridicule.'

'The existence and validity of human rights,' he continued 'are not written in the stars.'

America, the Land of the Free.

With the same foresight and intelligence with which he conducted his scientific life, Albert correctly predicted that a democratic Government would not survive acting the way it was.

But the narrow minded were outraged by this man's, a German Jew's, outspokenness. They felt that being granted American citizenship back in 1940 curtailed his right to oppose their Government's actions.

Complaints were made to the Director of the Institute for Advanced Study. 'This man needs lessons in Americanism,' wrote one enlightened woman.

'I suggest he move to Russia – and soon! We don't need him.' These words from a resident of New York.

However, the Director of the Institute, Robert Oppenheimer, had himself fallen victim to a McCarthy inquisition.

He remained full of support for his Professor.

Still, McCarthy's time was coming to an end. Finally, his lies surfaced and he was condemned for his 'contemptuous and reprehensible conduct.'

Just, a little too late for the many whose lives he had ruined.

It Albert Einstein did not directly bring about his downfall, then he played a significant role in its arrival.

McCarthy fell from grace and power in 1954, and by this time, although still a professor at the Institute in Princeton, he was living an increasingly secluded life.

On April 15th, 1955, he was admitted to hospital in Princeton with internal complaints.

Three days later, on April 18th, he died. Albert suffered an aortic aneurysm. He was 76 years of age.

The world had lost its greatest thinker. But more than that.

What Einstein knew was that intelligence was not the entire picture. He understood that difference between wisdom and intelligence.

He understood that intelligence without wisdom was deeply, deeply dangerous.

President Eisenhower paid tribute to the man.

He said: 'To all who live in the nuclear age, Albert Einstein exemplified the might creative ability of the individual in a free society.'

(There is a sad irony here that some of the research carried out for the chapter above included study of an article published by the Institute for Advanced Study.

This was written early in 2017 by a history working group from the institute.

They had been prompted to form by the decision of the Presidential Incumbent Donald Trump to ban travel and immigration from seven predominantly Muslim countries.

What would Albert Einstein have made of that?)

Albert Einstein's Legacies

Albert Einstein's scientific legacy is without precedence.

Even today, scientists are constantly discovering new facts which demonstrate the accuracy of his findings made at a time when Mankind simply did not possess the technology to be able to do more than hypothesize.

But his legacy extends well beyond his achievements in the world of Physics.

He made science popular. And fun. Generations of intellectuals have joined the world of scientific investigation because of the legacy of a wild haired old man fond of sticking his tongue out.

And as a result of this, more talent has entered the realm, and progressions in all fields of research have improved.

If that is possibly his greatest legacy, he also took science to a new level, linking a philosophy to it. He search for and belief in a unified world of physics in many ways echoed his beliefs in a unified people of the Earth.

He took science away from the mystical, and made sure it was based on facts. Whilst he would often theorize, he would need proof for those theories.

Such an approach is still held today – indeed it underpins virtually all research.

Many believe that his work inspired the artistic movement of Cubism. In this, objects are seen from numerous viewpoints; Einstein believed that physics should be seen from different perspectives.

His Theory of Relativity epitomizes such a stance.

It is claimed that his works inspired a generation of literary works, including those by William Faulkner.

His life also changed the public's view of the scientist in society. No longer could such a person be somebody who worked coldly outside of the needs of human kind.

Instead, a scientist needed a moral compass – a reason for working that would benefit the world.

And finally, his legacy is one of humanity. Humanity towards the down trodden, the discriminated against and those who are the victims of the powerful.

Right up to his death, he refused to accept any unjustified word of authority. He understood the importance of wisdom. And railed against those who did not possess it.

We should be thankful to him for that.

Conclusion

Albert Einstein, probably the greatest scientist the world has ever known, was awarded more than just the Nobel Prize in Physics.

In 1925, he was given the Copley Medal by the Royal Society; the Max Planck Medal from the German Physical Society followed in 1929.

The highest award of the French astronomical society, the Prix Jules Janssen was awarded tow hears later, and in 1934 he was chosen to give the Josiah Willard Gibbs lecture.

The Franklin Institute's Franklin Medal, from 1936, recognized his work on the photo electric effect and his research on relativity.

A century after his 'annus mirabilis, 2005, was declared World Year of Physics in honour of his discoveries.

Numerous institutions are named after him – The Albert Einstein College of Medicine is a research facility in the Bronx, New York and German has the Albert Einstein Science Park.

This contains the Einstein Tower, an observatory still finding further proofs of his theory of General Relativity. He has a memorial in Washington DC.

Chemical Element 99 is called 'einsteinium' and an asteroid is named in his honour.

He was identified, by none other than Time Magazine, as Person of the Century in 1999 and was named by his peers as the 'greatest physicist ever.'

He appears on a set of postage stamps and was inducted into the New Jersey Hall of

Fame. He appears on the Walhalla Temple, a memorial to 'laudable and distinguished Germans.'

The Albert Einstein Award or Medal recognizes high achievement in natural sciences. Another Albert Einstein Medal is awarded by the Albert Einstein Society in Bern.

But maybe, to this committed, lifelong pacifist, the greatest honour is the peace prize awarded annually in his name.

Not bad, for the son of a feather bed salesman.

Made in the USA
Columbia, SC
13 November 2018